U.S. SBN: 0-531-04182-4
Library of Congress
Catalog card No:
80-54726

Printed in Belgium

Published in the United
States
1981 by
Franklin Watts
730 Fifth Avenue
New York,
New York 10019

Strip-mining

COAL

BILL GUNSTON

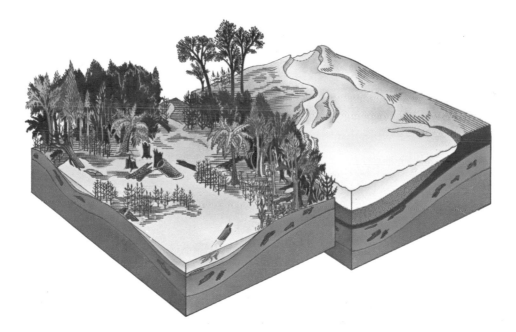

FRANKLIN WATTS

London · Toronto · New York · Sydney

Until recently mankind had taken energy for granted. It was always there – why bother about what it is or where it comes from? But today people are worried. Suddenly we discover that we have been using up important stores of energy – oil, natural gas and coal – far too quickly. We must all of us think very seriously: where will our energy come from in the future? For there is nothing in the world that is not affected by energy – or the lack of it – as this book and others in the series will show.

COAL – the fuel which enabled our modern industrialized society to emerge – is about to make a big come-back. For much of this century coal has been out of fashion. Its dominant position as an energy provider has been replaced by oil. But as a result of our energy problems and big oil price rises the world has come to recognize that coal is the most abundant fossil fuel. There is enough to last for hundreds of years and it can provide all of the main products now obtained from oil. As this book shows, in future coal mining will be a much more efficient, safer operation than in the past.

RAY DAFTER: *Consultant Editor*

Ray Dafter *is Energy Editor of the Financial Times. In 1978 he spent a year doing research at Harvard University, and lecturing in the United States. He has written two books on Energy, broadcasts on radio and television, and contributes to a number of publications.*

These are the world's energy sources. These can all be reached; some easily, others with rather more difficulty. The sun plays the principal role in this energy scheme. However, we do not at present use solar power in any great quantities – only indirectly. The sun nurtured all the plants and animals, that now millions of years later, we burn as fossil fuels – coal, oil and gas. We also use uranium to fuel nuclear power plants. It is impossible to replace some energy sources – but the sun, moon, wind and water are constant. These are the energy sources that will still be with us to tap in the future.

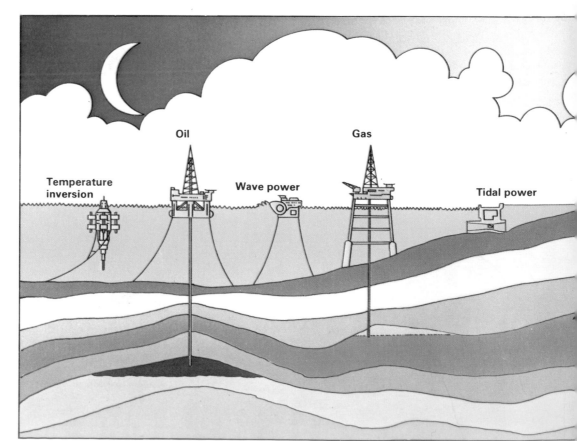

Temperature inversion   Oil   Wave power   Gas   Tidal power

Contents

The importance of coal	6
What is coal?	8
The search	10
Sinking a mine	12
Going down a mine	14
The long wall	16
Strip-mining	18
Old and new	20
Transporting coal	22
Coal power	24
Coal-based fuels	26
A wealth of products	28
Problems!	30
Latest developments	32
Future efficiency	34
Towards 2000!	36
Index	38

Art Director	Charles Matheson
Editor	Brian Sambrook
Art Editor	Ben White
Designer	David West
Typographic Design	Malcolm Smythe
Research	Dee Robinson
	Adam Martin

Illustrators

Denis Bishop	Moira Chesmur
Andrew Farmer	Jeremy Ford
Mike Gillah	Doug Harker
Gary Hincks	Peter Hutton
Industrial Art Studio	Jim Robins
Mike Tregenza	Brian Watson

Special thanks to 'Mining Magazine' for their co-operation in the production of this book.

For the purpose of this book:
A billion is one thousand million. A trillion is one million million.

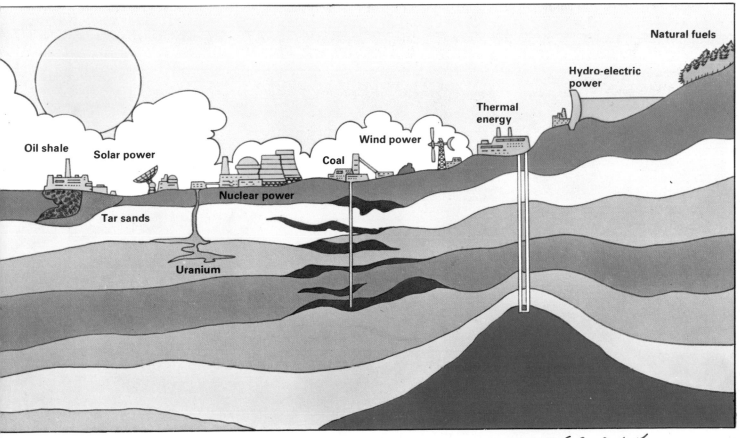

The importance of coal

Until quite recently, it was accepted that coal was moving steadily into decline as a major energy source. In the age of the jet, nuclear power and spaceflight it seemed old-fashioned, dirty and inefficient. Today, with oil becoming increasingly costly and scarce, and the demand for energy growing ever and ever greater, the mining industries of the world are being expanded in every possible way.

World coal production has doubled in the past 30 years to an annual total of almost 3.9 billion tons. More than one-fifth comes from the United States, nearly as much from the Soviet Union and only slightly less from China. Other important producers include East and West Germany, Poland and Great Britain. Such a wide distribution of coal fields across the world has naturally prompted further exploration, not only in established mining regions, but in places with no previous history of coal extraction. It is probable that before the end of the century we shall even be obtaining coal from far out at sea, as is already happening with oil and gas on a considerable scale.

▷ Coal is the most widespread fossil fuel. This map shows that both hard and soft coal is distributed throughout every continent of the world. Almost everywhere it is found, there are active mines. What the map cannot show – because it is not yet known – is how much coal lies beneath the sea. However, some of this coal is already being mined under the shallow continental shelves.

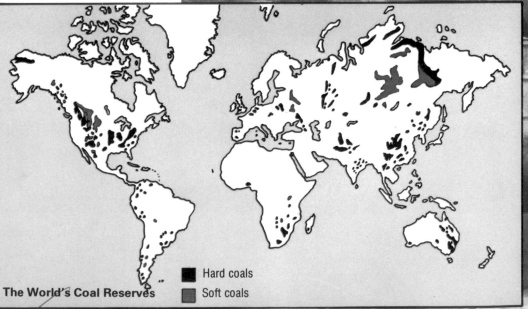

The World's Coal Reserves

■ Hard coals
▨ Soft coals

In the nineteenth century, most coal was used to power the industries of Europe and the United States. Today, it has a wider usage. For although the largest consumers are electricity power stations, closely followed by the world's iron and steel mills, one of the fastest growing uses of coal is as a source of valuable by-products. At present, petroleum, benzole, tars and synthetic rubbers are all being obtained from it.

At our current level of consumption, it is reckoned that the world's coal will last for about 200 years. This figure will of course be affected by increased rates of mining and consumption. On the other hand, new coal fields are being discovered, and improved technology will eventually enable us to mine coal which would otherwise have remained either unobtainable or not worth the cost of extraction.

◁ Electricity power stations require vast supplies of coal. Canada, a major coal supplier, exports a lot through the Roberts Bank Superport (above). The final journey to the power station is by train.

The scale on which coal is consumed is difficult to appreciate. If we imagine the world's tallest building – the Sears Roebuck tower in Chicago, which has a volume of 4.5 million m³ (159 million ft³) – filled six times over, we get an idea of the world's daily coal consumption.

◁ Coal is also of vital importance to the world steel industry – its second largest user. In Japan steel tops electricity for coal consumption, taking up 66 per cent of the total.

What is coal?

Coal is made up of three elements: carbon, hydrogen and oxygen. The proportions in which these elements are combined determine the type of coal. Broadly speaking, there are four main types: lignite, bituminous, cannel and anthracite. All four of these are the end products of a process of gradual decay and compression of plant material which began around 200 to 300 million years ago.

The first stage in the process is the creation of peat – a fossil fuel used as an important source of energy in its own right. Peat can form only a few hundred years after plant material has died. The decaying matter settles into a compact layer on the surface of the ground. Where, over longer periods, the peat is gradually buried and compressed, it becomes drier, harder and blacker. Peat which is transformed in this way is known as lignite, the softest (and incidentally the poorest burning) type of coal.

△ Imprints of leaves are often found in coal-bearing rock – evidence of coal's fossil origins.

△ Both peat and coal originate from swamp vegetation which flourished millions of years ago – most of it consisting of giant fern-like plants (1).

As the plants and trees died and crashed down they became covered by silt and mud, which gradually shaped them into a solid layer (2).

In the course of time, fresh forests appeared and disappeared into successive layers of peat. Over millions of years the layers sunk ever deeper, and under pressure from above, changed into coal (3).

◁ Most peat is cut by machines which compress the peat into neat bricks or sausage shapes. Finland and Ireland represent two of the major peat-producing countries.

◁ Movements in the Earth's crust create faults in the rock strata. These often break up the seams, creating problems for the miners trying to extract the coal.

Trough fault

Reverse fault

Step fault

Coal seam

◁ Lignite is normally found in relatively recent rocks. Most of it is consumed by power stations.

◁ Cannel coal probably got its name because thin pieces can be lit like a candle.

◁ Used in houses and factories, bituminous is the most popular of coals.

◁ Anthracite, the hardest coal of all, shows the most variation from the original peat beds.

When lignite becomes more deeply embedded in the Earth's crust, further changes occur. The accumulated weight of rock and earth above compact the lignite into the most common and varied coal-the bituminous type. This coal, made up of layers varying from bright and glassy to dull and sooty, is frequently found alongside a harder, more brittle type, known as cannel. Further compression, combined with the heat which such compression generates, causes some bituminous coal to change into anthracite, the hardest type of all. By this stage, all the hydrogen and oxygen have been squeezed out, leaving approximately 95 to 98 per cent carbon.

Coal is found in layers called seams. A seam 2 m (6½ ft) thick may once have been a 30-m (100-ft) thickness of peat. Many seams are thinner than this and broken up into a tangled arrangement at different levels by faults and earthquakes. Much of the Earth's coal is in seams so thin or irregular it cannot be economically mined.

The search

We do not know how or when it was first discovered that coal would burn. It is likely that the discovery was made by people who found coal in exposed seams – known as outcrops – by sea cliffs or on hillsides. Most of the world's coal, however, is found deep down in the layers of rock which form the Earth's crust, and requires sophisticated methods of detection and extraction.

Today, the search for coal is going on in almost every country. The mining companies involved employ geologists – people with expert knowledge of the Earth's rock formations – to locate new fields and attempt to determine their extent. To help them in their work, the geologists make use of a wide variety of extremely sensitive instruments.

Some of these instruments measure small changes in gravity or the Earth's magnetic field. More common is the use of seismograms. First, the ground is shaken by small explosions. The resulting sound waves travel down to the rock layers and bounce back to the surface where microphones pick them up. By noting the size of the explosion and the time the sound waves take to return, a picture of the rock layers below is obtained.

▷ Drill rigs used in searches for coal are similar to the drilling derricks which bore for oil and gas. Here a field engineer is carefully pulling out the core from one of the pieces of drill pipe bored through the different strata.

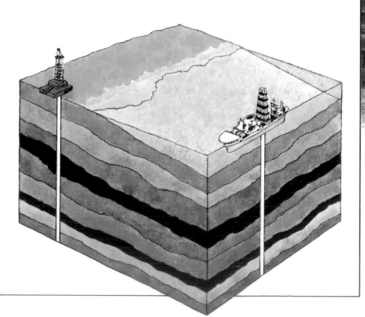

After geological surveys have indicated that coal may be present, the next task is to make test drillings. A pattern of drill sites is worked out and tubular drill pipes are then used to cut out a core. In this case one of the drill holes has been sunk offshore, though normally it is rare to drill farther than 8 km (5 miles) from the land.

◁ Where ships are used for offshore drilling, the drilling derrick – or tower – is positioned on the deck and the drill actually passes through the hull.

▽ The seismic method makes use of the fact that sound waves behave differently according to the density of the rocks through which they pass. Here we see waves pass through and bounce off the top and the bottom of a coal seam.

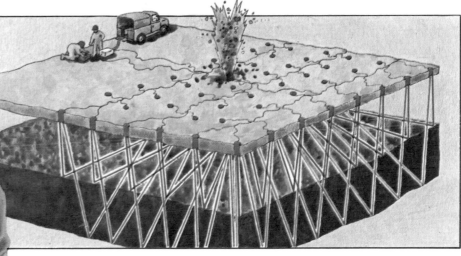

When the picture suggests that coal might be present, a test drilling is undertaken. A large rig is set up and a hollow tubular drill rotated into the ground. As the drill descends, fresh sections of drill pipe are added, and at intervals they are pulled out, bringing with them a central rod consisting of all the different rock layers – known as the core. The geologists study the core and take note of the exact depth and thickness of any coal which might have been found.

If the results are sufficiently encouraging, then further test drillings may be undertaken to discover the full extent of the coal field. Only then can a realistic assessment be made as to the viability of the find.

Sinking a mine

If a good, workable coal seam has been discovered and the location is considered suitable in terms of availability of labor and access to customers, the decision is taken to start a new mine. Today, this decision may also have to take account of opposition from local residents and conservationists. For, in the course of mining operations, the character and appearance of a region may be dramatically altered, sometimes to such an extent that the effects are permanent.

The first stage in establishing a new mine is to connect the coal seams to the surface. Seams may be found at any depth down to 1,300 m (4,250 ft), and often several seams are found at different depths within the same location. Two or more vertical or inclined shafts are sunk down to the coal seams. These shafts will be used for lowering the miners and equipment and to bring up the coal. Fresh air for the underground workers is forced down one of the shafts and stale air driven up the other by the action of large fans at the surface.

▽ As far as possible, the buildings used by the mine workers are kept separate from those which the coal passes through.

Surface offices, locker rooms and inspection rooms are all clustered around the winding tower, below which the upcast shaft lies.

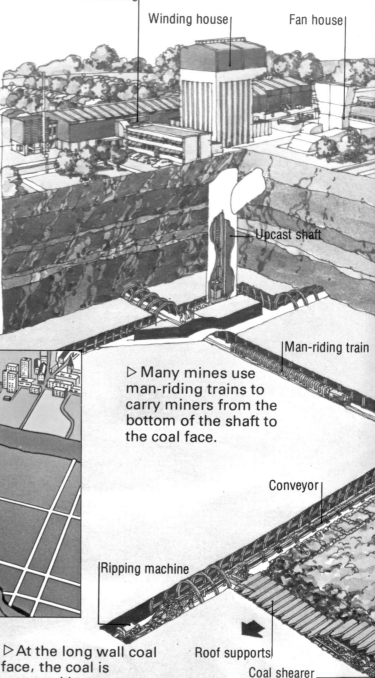

Surface Control building

Winding house

Fan house

Upcast shaft

Man-riding train

▷ Many mines use man-riding trains to carry miners from the bottom of the shaft to the coal face.

Conveyor

Ripping machine

Roof supports

Coal shearer

△ In long-established mines two or three layers of roadways and worked-out faces may be found, each extending over an area the size of a city.

▷ At the long wall coal face, the coal is removed by a rotary shearer loader connected to a row of roof supports.

▽ As coal arrives at the surface, it is tipped onto a conveyor belt. Normally the coal is carried directly to the preparation building. But where holdups occur in the preparation or shipment of the coal, this may not always be possible, and so the coal must be stored. Having arrived at the preparation plant, the coal is cleaned, washed and graded into several standard lump sizes for transportation.

From the base of the shafts a network of tunnels is dug. This may eventually cover anything up to 285 km² (110 square miles) and requires an extensive steel arch support system. The tunnels are used as roadways to convey men and machinery to and from the coal face. They also provide the route along which diesel and electric trains, or conveyors, carry coal to the shaft, and electric cables supply power to light the workings and operate the cutting and conveying machinery.

In Europe, the commonest method of cutting the coal is by "long wall" mining. This efficient method is normally performed by machines capable of removing an entire strip of coal from a seam, as they grind from one end of the coal face to the other.

Equipment yard

Coal storage

Winding house

Coal preparation plant

Loading bay

Coal train

Downcast shaft

Coal bunker

◁ At the downcast shaft fresh air from the surface comes in and freshly mined coal from the workings is carried out.

Main roadway

▽ Airflow in the mine is maintained by the constant action of powerful fans. Throughout the underground workings a breeze can be felt as the air circulates.

Goaf

△ Beside the roadways "gob" or "goaf" is built up into "pack" walls which support the roof in areas where the coal has been cut.

Pack

Supply train

➡ Stale air
➡ Fresh air

Going down a mine

◁ Dressed in protective gear and armed with equipment such as the Davy lamp (for detecting gas leaks), a group of workers descends the shaft by high-speed lift.

▽ At the pit bottom, a train takes the miners to the coal face. To pull the train, powerful diesel or electric locomotives are needed. These must be specially maintained to prevent them from giving off too many dangerous fumes and sparks.

Today, when miners go down into the depths of the Earth, they enter a world not unlike that of their predecessors: a world of darkness, dirt and danger. Though now the working areas are brightly lit, the rest of the mine remains unilluminated. Despite fresh air being drawn into the mine and foul and poisonous fumes sucked out, gas leaks are still a constant hazard.

Nonetheless, today's miners may go about their business with reasonable confidence. For in up-to-date mines conditions are monitored by the Surface Control room on data display, or closed-circuit television. Computer-linked instruments, too, provide continual information concerning production, breakdowns and the oxygen count in the mine. The workers can also keep in touch with each other by telephone and radio.

▷ The true nerve center of the modern mine is the Surface Control room. Here, information concerning all aspects of the work down below is received, assessed and acted upon. The introduction of computers has meant that even the underground conveyor system may be both monitored and controlled from above.

▷ With the aid of telephone and radio links, decisions affecting the day to day running of the mine may be quickly communicated to the coal face.

To help cope with the hardships of their daily routine, miners have also evolved a distinctive uniform and code of practice. As each man arrives for work, he changes from ordinary street clothes into special protective clothing. He collects a helmet and lamp which he attaches to the helmet, a freshly charged battery pack and steel-capped safety boots. Before entering the lift at the pithead, each miner is searched to make sure that he is not carrying a lighter or matches, which could be the cause of a fire or explosion in the mine. Each man also leaves behind a numbered disc. The disc is returned to him at the end of his shift. If a serious accident took place, it could be the only way of telling whether he was still down below.

Having reached the bottom of the shaft, it is usual for each miner to check with the foreman or deputy in charge of his work area to see what needs to be done. He then sets off to the coal face. In a large mine this may involve a journey of as much as 5 km (3 miles). Transport is normally provided by diesel locomotives. However, the miner sometimes has to walk the last half mile or so to the coal face, because the locomotives only travel along the main tunnels.

15

The long wall

In the advanced industrial countries more than 90 per cent of the coal from deep mines is cut by electric machines. Where the long wall method is used, the usual type of machine has a rotating cutter which resembles a circular saw, with hard teeth projecting from a drum. Shaving off the coal like a meat slicer in a delicatessen, the cutter, mounted on an AFC (armored face conveyor), moves along from one end of the face to the other dragged by powerful chains which are attached to a winch.

Complementing the cutting machine and AFC is an impressive system of roof supports. In most modern mines these consist of a tightly packed row of upright hydraulic jacks, arranged in groups of up to four, which press upwards on strong steel beams that hold up the roof. Altogether, they are able to exert a force of tens of thousands of tons.

As the cutter advances along the face, the supports are moved up to the freshly cut face behind it. The pressure in each support is in turn released, allowing the beam to come down out of contact with the roof. Then horizontal rams thrust it forward up to the new line of the face, where it is again put under pressure to hold up the roof. Meanwhile, the roof of the area vacated by the supports is allowed to collapse behind them, the debris which is subsequently left behind being known as "goaf."

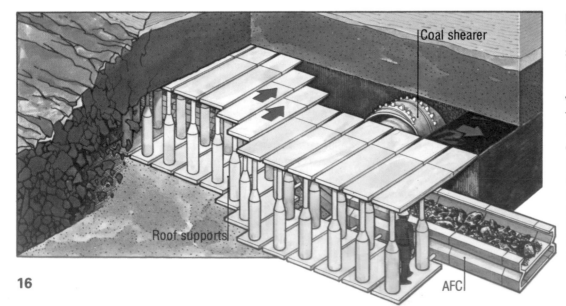

Roof supports

Coal shearer

AFC

In most mines the coal is won by a machine such as this shearer loader, whose teeth rotate on a drum from which water is sprayed to keep down dust. As it eats through the coal, hydraulic rams push on the AFC, to move it up to the newly cut face. The roof supports move in behind the shearer to hold up the exposed roof.

As the coal is cut, it drops on to the AFC, which transports it to a conveyor belt supported on rollers. This conveyor, positioned at one end of the coal face and sprinkled with water to keep down the coal dust, carries the coal to the foot of the shaft. From there it is transferred to large buckets known as skips, which are then hoisted to the surface and there deposit the coal onto another conveyor.

As the coal face advances, the tunnels on either side of the coal-winning face must be extended. This work involves powerful ripping machines tearing out the rock, or alternatively, high-precision drills may be used to bore holes into which small explosives are then placed.

△ In tunneling operations using explosives, hydraulic drills bore very precise holes to ensure an even blast.

Strip-mining

Where coal seams reach the surface and "out-crop" or where they lie at relatively shallow depths, it is possible to extract the coal without working under the ground. The method employed is called strip-mining; the soil and rock lying on the surface above the coal – known as over-burden – are simply stripped off to reveal the seam beneath.

Stripping off the overburden and mining the coal is usually done by mechanical excavator shovels which load into dump trucks for trans-port to the preparation plant or railhead. Other methods involve draglines or bucket wheel excavators. With draglines a loading bucket skims across the surface, drawn by steel chains or cables. Bucket wheel excavators, or BWEs, have a series of toothed buckets fitted to the rim of a revolving wheel which is moved upwards and along the rock or coal face.

In the lignite mines between Cologne and Aachen in West Germany, there are enormous seams which are being dug out by the strip-mining method using bucket wheel excavators. The machines used are gigantic, each weighing as much as 15,000 tons.

▽ The size and capacity of modern strip-mining machines is vast. This 13,000-ton BWE digs 200,000 m³ (700,000 ft³) daily.

Bucket Wheel Excavator

Such is the scale of this operation that whole villages have had to be demolished and rebuilt at new sites to make way for the advancing machinery. To date, 24,280 persons have been resettled in the Cologne–Aachen area (not to mention countless other souls whose coffins have been dug up and transplanted to new village cemeteries!)

Accompanying this mass movement of people and materials is the equally daunting process of reclamation – creating a totally new landscape of farms, hills and roads. In parts of the United States the mining and reclamation are almost simultaneous. For as soon as a coal strip has been removed, the resulting trench is promptly refilled with overburden. The topsoil is then replaced, and within a year crops may well be growing on the land.

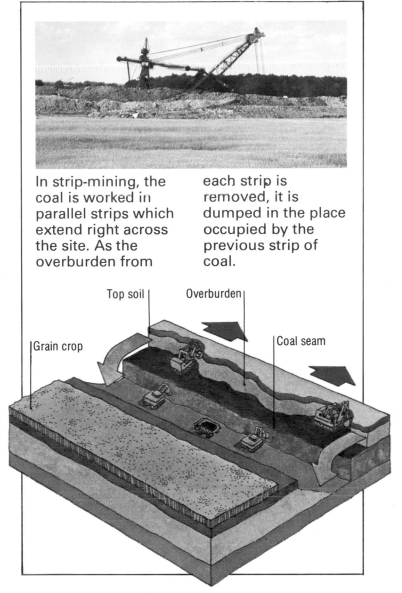

In strip-mining, the coal is worked in parallel strips which extend right across the site. As the overburden from each strip is removed, it is dumped in the place occupied by the previous strip of coal.

Top soil | Overburden

Grain crop | Coal seam

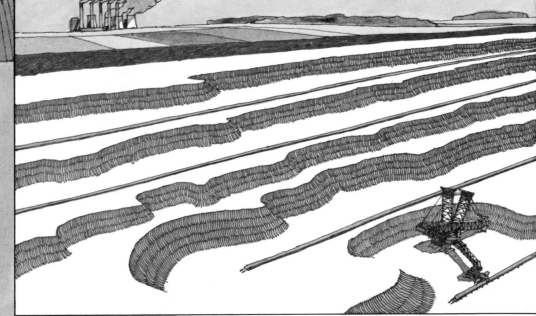

▷ In the massive strip-mining sites of West Germany coal beds extend over an area of 2,500 km² (965 square miles). BWEs, giant stackers and large interconnected in-pit conveyors work around the clock cutting and stacking overburden, removing coal and replacing the overburden. The site resembles a series of vast terraces.

Old and new

The world's leading coal producer is the United States. In some respects, such as development of mining machines, new strip-mining methods and coal transportation, the United States leads the field. Yet most of its deep mining is done by one of the oldest established mining methods, known as room and pillar.

Continuous miner machines drive straight ahead to the end of the working section. After cutting a series of parallel corridors through the coal, another series of cuts is made at right angles. The result is that about half the coal is left behind as square pillars supporting the roof. Sometimes these pillars are left standing. More often, they are mined in the second working.

In the Soviet Union and Poland most deep mining is performed using a form of long wall mining called the retreat method. Here, two parallel tunnels are bored directly to the end of the seam. Then they are linked with a crosscut. The miners work back or retreat toward the mine entrance, taking out the coal between the tunnels.

A major advantage of retreat mining is that the seam's quality and depth are known before coal is produced in any quantity. Another is that the complete conveyor system can be installed at the outset. On the other hand, such extensive development requires greater initial expenditure than in conventional long wall mining, and means a slower return on investment.

View from below of Room and Pillar mine

Room and pillar is a fast method of mining which dispenses with conventional roof supports. Though virtually obsolete in Europe, it has persisted in American mines where modern techniques and equipment have been incorporated.

▷ To the right, we see two of the more sophisticated pieces of equipment used in modern room and pillar mines: the continuous miner used to cut the coal, and the gathering arm loader which helps in the removal of coal from the mine.

◁ In some countries, miners still cut the coal with picks and load it into tubs with shovels. Wooden roof supports, as seen in the entrance to this Nigerian mine, are another feature which persists in some parts. Probably in the near future, labor will become increasingly expensive and machines will virtually take over completely.

A simplified plan of retreat mining, where two access roads have been driven from the shaft to the edge of the face and the coal between them is now being extracted by working back.

Roadway

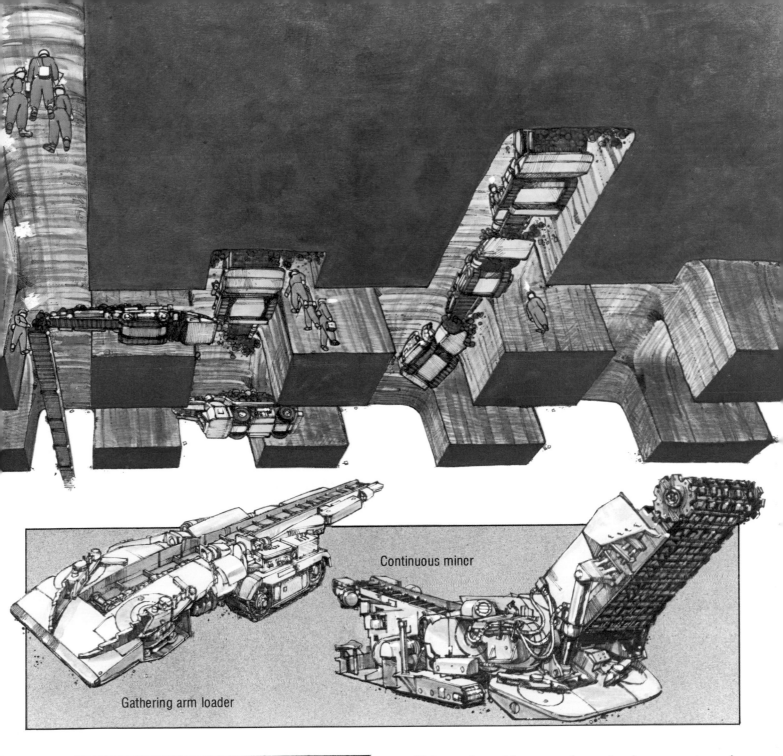

Continuous miner

Gathering arm loader

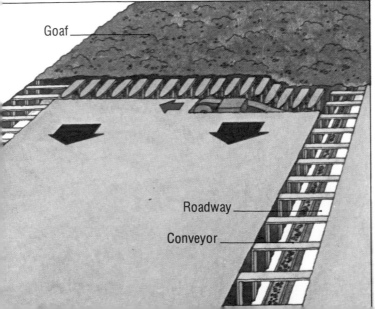

Goaf

Roadway

Conveyor

China, the oldest coal-producing country, is today undergoing a massive expansion of its mining operations. Strip-mines, room and pillar and long wall are all being developed there using the latest technology and equipment, much of it imported from the West.

In Australia, where huge deposits of both lignite and high-quality bituminous coal have been found, most mining is done by the strip method. At present, more than half the continent's coal is exported, the main customer being Japan, though Europe is also taking considerable amounts.

Transporting coal

Each day more than 11 million tons of coal is carried away from the world's mines. Between 5 and 10 per cent is exported by sea, mainly in large ships called bulk carriers. In countries such as the Soviet Union, West Germany and the United States coal barges are a common sight on canals and rivers.

Overland, trains designed specifically for the job provide the main form of coal transport. Up to 100 hopper cars, each with a capacity of about 100 tons, are permanently coupled together and spend their entire life shuttling between mine and coal user. Britain pioneered the merry-go-round technique in which, at each end of the line, cars are automatically loaded or emptied without the train ever actually coming to rest. The Black Mesa & Lake Powell railroad in the United States. has even developed a train whose operations are completely computer-controlled.

◁ On the inland waterways of Europe and the USA coal is transported by boats ranging from small flat-bottom lighters to 20,000-ton barges. This huge barge is docked on one of Germany's busy canals. In the foreground is an automatic conveyor loader.

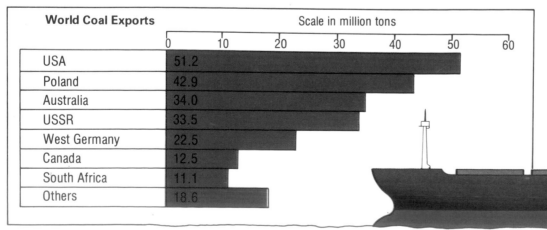

World Coal Exports	Scale in million tons
	0 10 20 30 40 50 60
USA	51.2
Poland	42.9
Australia	34.0
USSR	33.5
West Germany	22.5
Canada	12.5
South Africa	11.1
Others	18.6

◁ Exports of coal depend on the balance between a country's coal production and its requirements. The United States happens to have a surplus of coal, but this could change.

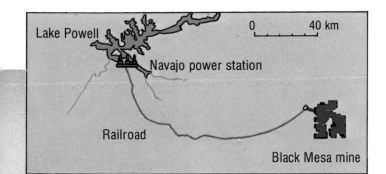

The enormous expenditure on track, rolling stock and terminal equipment, however, makes rail transport over vast distances less attractive, and in the United States alternative means are being tried and tested. Pumping coal along pipelines is one.

Specially prepared coal is first crushed into powder, and then mixed with water in roughly equal proportions, to form what is known as "slurry". The slurry is then pumped along the pipelines at speeds fast enough to prevent the coal particles from settling.

In most of the coal slurry pipelines, the ideal velocity is about 6 km/h (4 mph). However, when the pipeline crosses rough and mountainous terrain, pumping pressure may need to be boosted considerably to maintain this velocity. The Black Mesa pipeline, which extends from near Kayenta Arizona to the borders of Nevada, is just such a case. Accordingly, it is equipped with four pump stations at intervals along its 440-km (273-mile) route.

◁ The Black Mesa & Lake Powell railroad links a coal mine in Arizona, USA, with a power station. Two computerized electric trains make six round trips a day on the 128-km (78-mile) route.

▽ Nearly all the coal exported over long distances travels by sea. Coal is a bulk cargo, which means that it is stored loose in the holds of ships rather like oil tankers.

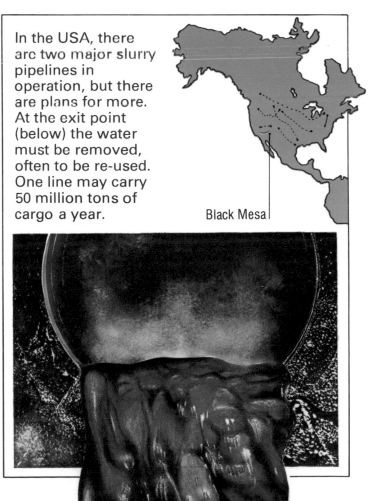

In the USA, there are two major slurry pipelines in operation, but there are plans for more. At the exit point (below) the water must be removed, often to be re-used. One line may carry 50 million tons of cargo a year.

Black Mesa

Coal power

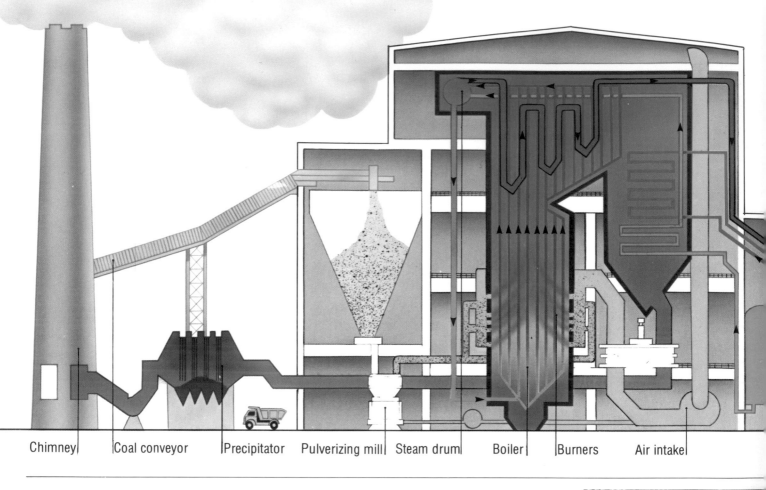

Chimney | Coal conveyor | Precipitator | Pulverizing mill | Steam drum | Boiler | Burners | Air intake

Electricity generating stations– these are the main destination for most of the world's coal supplies. Wherever possible, the coal-fired power stations are built beside coal fields. It is much faster and cheaper to transport electricity than coal. Huge cables extending over many miles simply feed it into a grid system, which directs the power to wherever it is needed. This efficient use of coal is known as "coal by wire".

All the modern coal-fired power stations burn pulverized coal. Usually the coal is crushed at the power station and blown by powerful jets of hot air into the boilers where it burns in towering flames of up to 40 m (130 ft) – approximately as high as a ten-story building.

In the largest power stations, there may be as many as six boilers, with a combined coal-burning capacity in excess of 10 million tons a year.

△The modern steam boiler is a most imposing machine. Some use oil or nuclear fuel, but most are fed with coal pulverized on site. The fuel is carried by conveyor belt to a bunker from which it falls into the pulverizing mill. From the mill, it is blown with hot air jets into the boiler where burners set it on fire.

▷ A massive turbine generator stands out clearly in the turbine hall of the Drax (UK) power station.

▽Within the boiler, tubes extending to the full height of the structure are subjected to tremendous heat. The temperature of the water circulating through the tubes (colored blue) is immediately raised, creating steam (colored red) which is subsequently passed through a superheater and on to the turbines. From the turbines the steam flows into a condenser.

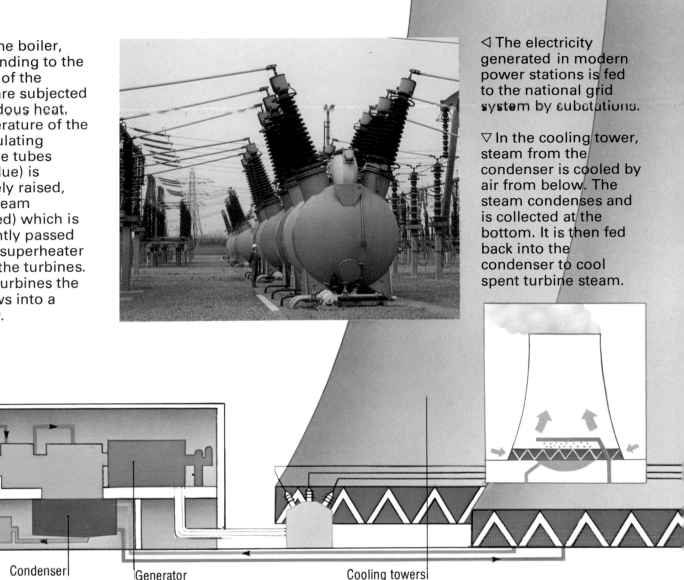

◁ The electricity generated in modern power stations is fed to the national grid system by substations.

▽ In the cooling tower, steam from the condenser is cooled by air from below. The steam condenses and is collected at the bottom. It is then fed back into the condenser to cool spent turbine steam.

Turbine   Condenser   Generator   Cooling towers

Inside each boiler, water is turned to steam in reinforced steel tubes. These tubes are fed with cold water at the rate of about 150 litres/sec (32 Imp gal/sec). The water circulates through the heated tubes until it turns to steam. Even hotter tubes increase the temperature of the steam, until finally at the outlet – where the steam pipe glows white hot – it is released at enormous pressure into the first turbine. This high-pressure turbine, consisting of hundreds of blades like small wings mounted on a spinning drum, revolves furiously as the steam hits it.

The steam, having returned to the boiler for reheating, progresses to an intermediate turbine with larger blades. Finally, steam at reduced pressure is released into a giant turbine with enormous blades. All three turbines are connected to a shaft powering an electric generator.

Coal-based fuels

▽ White-hot coke is rammed out of a coke oven into a spray of cold water. Though wasteful in terms of heat, this is the only way coal can be turned into hard coke (almost pure carbon) for the world's steel industry.

Every lump of coal is today recognized as a storehouse of valuable carbon and hydrogen, from which several important fuels and innumerable by-products can be made. One of the most important fuels is petroleum. Using the Lurgi process, crushed coal is first mixed with steam and oxygen to obtain methane. To create the liquid hydrocarbons from which petroleum is formed, the methane is then combined with hydrogen atoms.

This process, originally perfected by the German chemists Fischer and Tropsch, was in use during World War II among countries in desperate need of alternative fuel supplies. Today, with oil-based fuels soaring in price, it represents both a valuable lifeline for the present and a reassuring prospect for the future. Indeed, the Sasol Corporation is fast making South Africa independent of oil imports by converting its abundant coal reserves into petroleum.

△ In a blast furnace the coke, once more white-hot, reacts with iron to form molten slag which absorbs impurities from the steel. The steel is run off in a bright liquid stream each time the furnace is "tapped". Coke is also the chief source of the carbon in steel.

While coal cooked to white heat gives us the fuel known as coal gas, this has been largely replaced by natural gas. Nevertheless, the process of cooking coal remains a valuable means of obtaining fuels. For apart from releasing gas, it leaves behind the solid residue which we know as coke.

Without coke there would be no steel industry. Within that industry it performs three essential functions in the metal-making furnace. It supplies the heat needed to melt the iron and limestone from which steel is formed. It removes the oxygen from the iron ore, and while strong enough to support the "burden" (the mix of ingredients), it is still porous enough to allow hot gases to escape.

As a fuel used in the home, coke – like other smokeless fuels – has the added advantage of burning more cleanly than coal. Accordingly, in advanced industrial countries where it is against the law to have a visibly smoky chimney, it has become very popular.

△ In this pilot plant at Baytown, Texas, coal is reacted with steam to form methane and carbon dioxide in the production of SNG (substitute natural gas). Huge storage tanks are in the background.

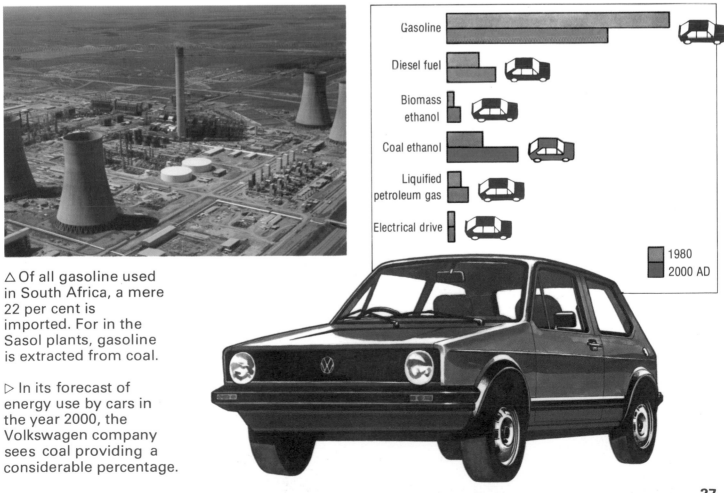

△ Of all gasoline used in South Africa, a mere 22 per cent is imported. For in the Sasol plants, gasoline is extracted from coal.

▷ In its forecast of energy use by cars in the year 2000, the Volkswagen company sees coal providing a considerable percentage.

Gasoline
Diesel fuel
Biomass ethanol
Coal ethanol
Liquified petroleum gas
Electrical drive

1980
2000 AD

A wealth of products

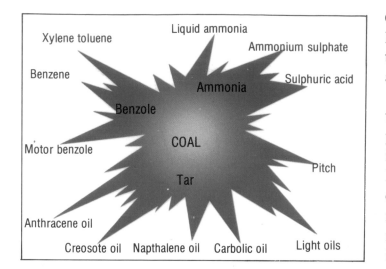

Xylene toluene
Liquid ammonia
Ammonium sulphate
Benzene
Sulphuric acid
Ammonia
Benzole
Motor benzole
COAL
Pitch
Tar
Anthracene oil
Light oils
Creosote oil   Napthalene oil   Carbolic oil

Coal gases not only form the basis from which liquid hydrocarbons such as petroleum are made, they are also the source of such useful substances as coal tar, benzole and ammonia.

Almost all the common waterproofing materials such as road tar, bitumen, asphalt and pitch originate from coal tars. So do some roofing materials and damp-courses for buildings. Benzole, though used as a fuel, usually goes to the chemical industry for processing into paints, medicines, soaps and detergents. Ammonia, commonly known as a poisonous gas, can be used in the manufacture of explosives and fertilizers.

Other products which may be derived from coal liquids include synthetic rubbers and floor coverings. Further sophisticated processing gives us more than 400 plastics, including such fibers as nylon and terylene and such everyday products as lighter fuel, adhesives and the basis of photographic film.

△ The smoke produced when coal is burned as a fuel contains many chemical substances which are normally wasted. When coal is heated during the coke-making operation this volatile matter is recovered and further processed to produce materials for use in a wide range of industries.

▽ Many of today's household goods can be obtained from coal. Some, such as coal tar soaps, have been around for many years. Others, like detergents and packaging materials, are newcomers.

In building a house it is virtually impossible to avoid using coal-based materials. These include breeze blocks, damp-courses, wood preservatives, roofing felt and tarmacadam. Later, rust preventative, adhesives, floor coverings and paint – all derived from coal – may be used in the interior decoration.

At present, many of the products we have mentioned are also petroleum-based. But as the price of oil shoots up, an intensified search is being conducted to discover ways of switching the source material from oil to coal.

There is nothing we get from oil that cannot be made from coal – from the fuel we use to run our vehicles, down to the artificial sweeteners we put in tea and coffee. Moreover, present-day research into ways of extending our use of the "waste" products derived from burning coal has also proven very successful.

Already, the ash from coal-burning power stations is being put to extensive use. This fine grey powder known as PFA (pulverized fuel ash) makes an excellent base material for building roadways. It can also be spread on the ground as a safety measure to stop aircraft which have run off airport runways. In a coarser form, pulverized fuel ash is made into rough "breeze blocks" which are frequently used for the interior walls of modern houses and flats.

▽ Several types of insulator and wrapping used in electric cables can be obtained from coal. So, too, can printing ink and some photographic film. Explosives derived from ammonia provide another outlet.

Farming provides rich opportunities for expanding the use of coal. Such essentials as pesticides for crop spraying, weed-killers, fertilizers, and even animal feed are all potential coal-based products. At present, the main source is oil, but efforts are being made to switch to coal.

Blasting with explosives

29

Problems!

Although the efficiency of coal use is today greatly improved, there remain quite considerable problems. Coal is still black and dirty, and burning or processing it causes pollution from smoke and soot, unless expensive filtering and washing processes are used.

Despite advances in mining, too, the extraction of coal cannot be carried out without some risk to miners from roof falls, flooding, explosions and gas leaks. Mining accidents are rarer than they used to be, but even in the very best and most safety conscious mines, miners can still be killed or seriously injured, often because of a single moment's carelessness.

The dangers of mining, moreover, are not confined to below the surface. Where coal is extracted from a mine and the roof collapses, each successive layer above begins to break up. This chain reaction, known as subsidence, causes the land on the ground surface to sag, which in turn puts a severe strain on buildings and structures in the vicinity. Houses have been known to collapse under such stress. One solution is to leave pillars of coal unmined, in a similar fashion to the traditional room and pillar method.

Another environmental problem arising from extensive mining is the disposal of waste. Up until quite recently, it was simply piled into slag heaps. At Aberfan, Wales, in 1966, a huge slag heap of colliery waste softened by rains suddenly avalanched down to bury 144 people, most of them children and teachers in a nearby school. Today, such unsightly and dangerous mounds are being removed – often yielding thousands of tons of coal in the process.

Concern for "loss of amenity" has also prompted a positive response to the problem of healing the giant scars caused by strip mining. Often this involves depositing as much as a million tons of soil, planting trees, grass and crops. Like the washing and filtering of power station smoke it can be done, but it costs money, which in effect makes coal more expensive. Today, we are more prepared to pay the price.

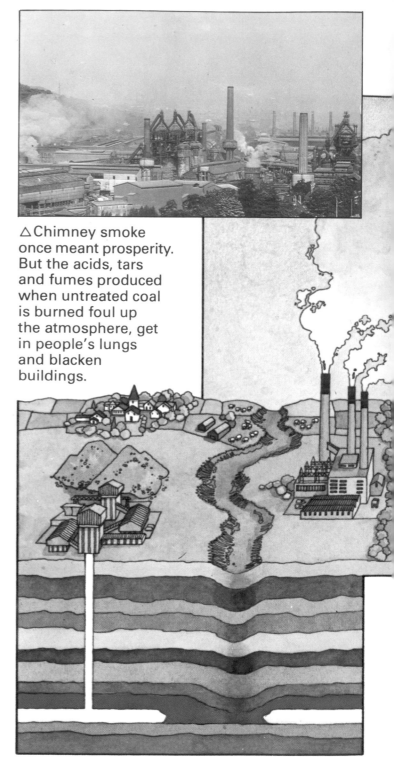

△ Chimney smoke once meant prosperity. But the acids, tars and fumes produced when untreated coal is burned foul up the atmosphere, get in people's lungs and blacken buildings.

△ Until recently, mines piled unwanted waste in slag heaps. Taking years to settle down, these smoldering heaps were a source of pollution.

△ Subsidence is often taken into account when planning the thickness of coal to be extracted and the proportions to be worked in a mine.

All combustion on the Earth is bound to degrade energy to heat, which tends to upset the basic heat balance of the planet – even if only very slowly.

▷ According to some scientists, dust particles produced by burning coal can form smog high up in the atmosphere. The smog keeps out sunlight, thus cooling the Earth.

Sun's reflected heat

▽ Various materials, such as sulphur dioxide and trioxide from coal fires, are carried from one country to another and mix with water to rain weak acid.

Another theory is that carbon dioxide builds up in the atmosphere and keeps heat in, gradually causing a heat excess which could melt polar ice and cause floods.

Reflected heat

Acid rain

△ In countries where the dumping of colliery waste is still legal, inestimable damage is done to water plants, insect life and spawning grounds.

△ A working strip-mine will inevitably spoil the landscape. Afterwards though, the huge pits created can be made into recreational lakes.

Latest developments

△ The hydraulic cutter operates from tunnels drilled into the seam. The machine retreats, cutting as shown, and continues until the roof collapses. This process is repeated for each tunnel.

Inclined coal seam ─

What are the immediate objectives of mining? One is to obtain coal and its by-products as cheaply and efficiently as possible. Another is to reduce accidents to miners. And finally, we require more coal to be dug. We should not forget that, at present, most of the coal in the Earth's crust has to be ignored because it is in seams too thin, too jumbled or too scattered to be worth the cost of extraction.

Most of the present-day advances in mining involve better ways of cutting and removing the coal. One of the most promising is hydraulic mining. This system, tested in West Germany and perfected in an experimental mine in British Columbia, involves the directing of a high-pressure water jet on to an inclined coal seam. The resulting coal and water slurry is then allowed to flow by means of gravity out of the mining area and down into a preparation plant where it is separated out.

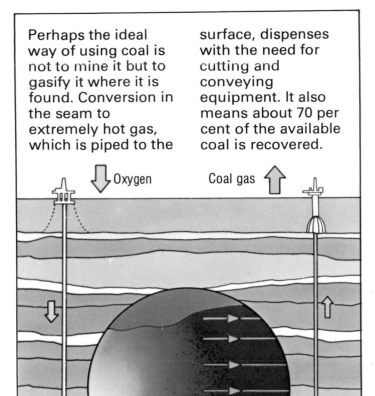

Perhaps the ideal way of using coal is not to mine it but to gasify it where it is found. Conversion in the seam to extremely hot gas, which is piped to the surface, dispenses with the need for cutting and conveying equipment. It also means about 70 per cent of the available coal is recovered.

Oxygen

Coal gas

Where inclined coal seams are not present, removing the slurry produced by hydraulic mining becomes something of a problem. One solution has been to introduce flexible pipelines. In this way the coal slurry can be pumped to an underground collection point from where it is injected into a rigid pipeline for transportation to the surface.

The hydraulic slurry transport system is also being taken up in mines where advanced versions of the continuous miner are used. For, with a capacity for removing coal far outstripping conventional transporting systems, it is well able to cope with the 10 tons a minute which these powerful new machines can rip from a coal seam.

One advanced mining scheme dispensing with the need for coal transport altogether is underground gasification. Here, holes are drilled into the seam, which is then set on fire. As the coal burns, it releases gases which are then piped to the surface for collection and distribution. This system has obvious applications in places where conventional mining methods are unsuitable.

◁ A futuristic impression of an advanced continous miner, equipped with hydraulic slurry pipes. With a coal-cutting capacity equivalent to ten men working flat out, such machines need a fast and efficient transport system.

Water

Coal slurry

Power cables

Future efficiency

Discounting coal as an important fuel for modern-day use was one of the biggest mistakes the experts ever made. Today, oil has shot up in price and the expansion of nuclear power is being checked by both political and technical problems. The world's coal output, on the other hand, is expected to continue increasing as far into the future as we can reasonably predict.

Nevertheless, our proven coal reserves are by no means inexhaustible. For this reason it is important that ways are found of burning coal more effectively.

In a modern power station only about 33 per cent of the heat produced by burning coal is put to use, with approximately two-thirds of the heat escaping up the chimney or being wasted in the condenser. A new plant built in Rivesville, West Virginia has achieved an immediate improvement to 50 per cent using a multi-cell fluidized bed combustion boiler – the first of its kind to be built anywhere in the world.

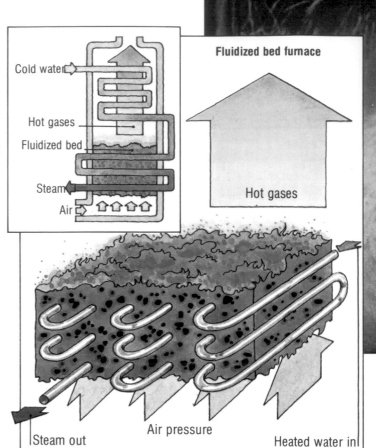

Cold water

Hot gases

Fluidized bed

Steam

Air

Fluidized bed furnace

Hot gases

Steam out

Air pressure

Heated water in

△ By having the water or steam-raising tubes situated in the bed of hot sand, approximately half of the heat generated in the FBC is absorbed directly. The remainder of the FBC's steam output results from the recovery of the combustion gases in the conventional part of the boiler above the furnace.

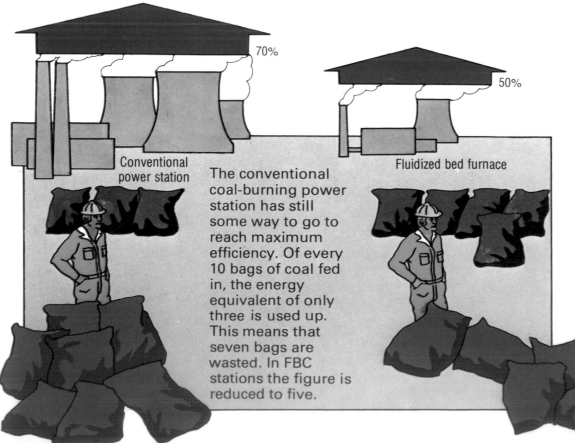

70%

50%

Conventional power station

Fluidized bed furnace

The conventional coal-burning power station has still some way to go to reach maximum efficiency. Of every 10 bags of coal fed in, the energy equivalent of only three is used up. This means that seven bags are wasted. In FBC stations the figure is reduced to five.

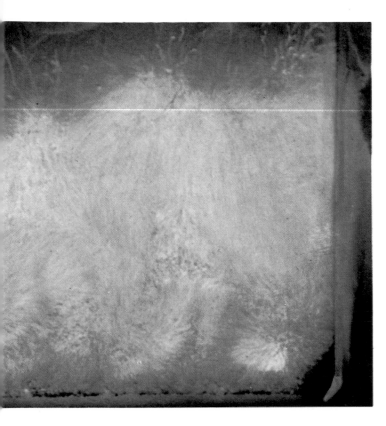

The fluidized bed boiler works by means of coal being piped into a hot churning bed of sand. In this way, the red-hot sand, kept in motion by a current of air blown from the bed of the boiler, mixes continually with the coal, thereby ensuring that it burns very efficiently. This means that the supply of heat to the steam-raising tubes is also improved, which in turn increases the general efficiency of electrical generation.

While maximizing the extraction of heat the system also ensures minimal discharges of pollution. For, mixed in with the sand and coal, are particles of limestone. These particles chemically react with the poisonous sulphur dioxide produced when coal is burned, thereby trapping it before it can escape.

In the field of transport, too, there are plans for pollution-free and efficient coal use in the boilers of a new breed of steam locomotives. Unlike the picturesque but wasteful locomotives of the past, these future ones will be capable of continuously recycling their steam along cooling pipes connected to the boilers, which themselves burning low-grade smokeless coal.

△ In this experimental version of the FBC, the sand and coal mixture is churned round and round by means of powerful jets of air which are blown from below.

Coal-powered Locomotive

▷ Trains such as this may soon herald a new age of steam. The boiler is housed in a separate unit containing a special coal bunker underneath. The steam generated in the boiler passes into the power unit of the locomotive to power a drive unit.

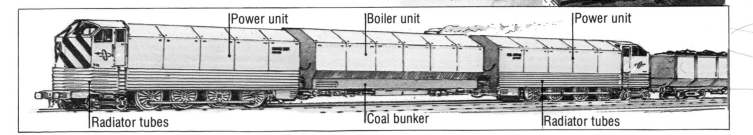

Power unit   Boiler unit   Power unit

Radiator tubes   Coal bunker   Radiator tubes

Toward 2000!

As our reliance upon coal increases, a number of difficulties must be overcome if our way of life is to be safeguarded and indeed perpetuated. One obvious problem is to ensure that pollution levels are held in check, and wherever possible improved. At the same time, we must seek more efficient ways of converting coal into energy, while making certain that the recovery of valuable by-products is also maximized.

In the past, none of these problems was satisfactorily dealt with. Indeed, with the discovery of oil as a more efficient, convenient and pollution-free source of energy and materials, many governments simply turned their backs on coal, or at least relegated it to the position of a second-rate fuel. Today, with oil reserves fast running out, we are forced to take a more positive approach.

One step in the right direction is the proposed establishment, close to mines, of integrated plants which are at once factories, heating plants and power stations. Such plants are called coalplexes .

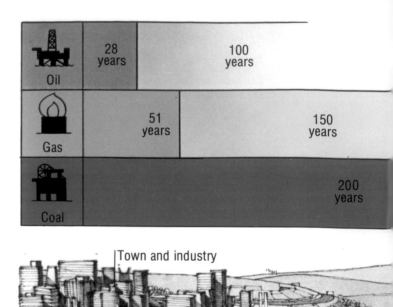

Oil	28 years	100 years
Gas	51 years	150 years
Coal		200 years

▷ In the mining towns of the near future we will see an integration in both the appearance and activities of the various component parts. At the mine, the pithead gear and surface works will be totally enclosed and designed to merge with the architecture of the neighboring coalplex and commercial installations. These installations, including gas stations, market gardens, steel works and power stations, will be serviced by an integrated transport system handling both raw materials from the mine and finished products from the coalplex.

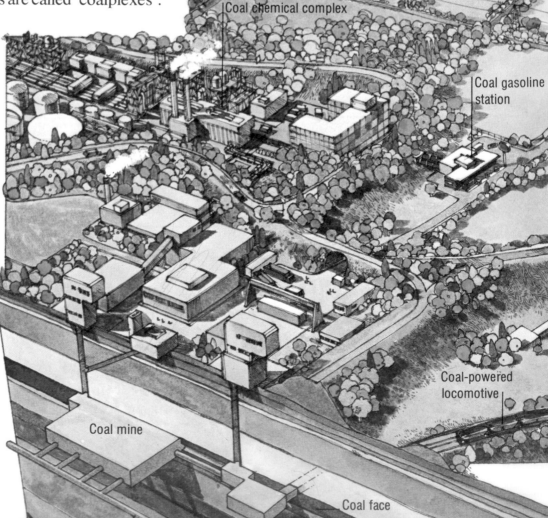

Town and industry

Coal chemical complex

Coal gasoline station

Coal-powered locomotive

Coal mine

Coal face

The Earth's reserves of recoverable oil and gas are expected to last 28 and 51 years respectively. With improved recovery methods these figures may reach 100 and 150 years. But they still fall short of coal which has proven reserves of 200 years and the potential to last 1,000-3,000 years.

1000-3000 years

There are many ways in which coalplexes might be arranged. In some schemes the incoming coal would be divided between ovens, fluidized bed boilers and other installations for making oil and gasoline. In others, the coal may be crushed, then cooked in ovens, and the hot gases used both to give oils and other products. Alternatively, the segregation of the coal might take place within the mine itself. Clean coal, required for purposes such as coke making, would be separated from coal of lower quality which would be used as power station fuel. Any crushing required in this process would take place underground.

With the linking of coal mines and coalplex plants a new form of industrial center will be created. Around this center new towns will flourish not only utilizing the power and finished products from the coalplex, but taking full advantage of waste heat for the direct heating of their commercial, industrial and domestic installations. Unlike the mining communities of the past, built solely to service the mine, those of the future shall exist to reap its benefits.

Farm

Fluidized bed power station

Market garden

Steel industry

Index

A
Aachen 18, 19
Aberfan 30
accidents 15, 30
anthracite 8, 9
armoured face conveyor
  (AFC) 16, 17
Australia 21

B
bituminous coal 8, 9, 21
Black Mesa pipeline 23
Black Mesa & Lake Powell
  railway 22
British Columbia 32
bucket wheel excavators
  (BWEs) 18
by-products 7, 26, 28-9, 32,
  36

C
Canada 7
cannel coal 8, 9
carbon 8, 9, 26
China 21
coal barges 22
coal face 12, 13, 14, 15, 16,
  17
coal fields 7, 10, 11
coal gas 27, 28
coalplexes 36-7
coke 26, 27, 28
Cologne 18, 19
computers 14, 15, 22, 23
continuous miner 20, 33
conveyor(s) 13, 18
  belt 12, 15, 17, 24
  loader 22
  system 15, 21

D
Davy lamp 14
draglines 18
drill(s) 11
  high-pressure 17
  hydraulic 16
drill holes 10
drill pipes 10, 11
drill rigs 10, 11

drilling 10
  derricks 11
  test 11

E
East Germany 6
electricity 24, 25
  generating stations 24
  power stations 7, 24, 25,
  30, 34
energy 6, 27, 34, 36
Europe 7, 13, 20, 21, 22
explosives 16, 17, 28, 29

F
Finland 9
Fischer and Tropsch 26
fluidized bed combustion
  (FBC) 34-5, 37
fossil fuels 6, 8
fuels 26-7, 34

G
gas 6, 27, 37
  leaks 14, 30
gasification 33
gathering arm loader 20
geologists 10, 11
"goaf" 13, 16
"gob" 13, 30
Great Britain 6, 22

H
hydraulic mining 32-3
hydrogen 8, 9, 26

I
Ireland 9
iron ore 27
iron mills 7

J
Japan 7, 21

L
lignite 8-9, 18, 21
locomotives 35
  diesel 14, 15
  electric 14

steam 35
  see also trains
long wall mining 13, 16-7,
  20, 21
Lurgi process 26

M
mining 6, 7, 12, 21, 30, 32
  see also hydraulic,
  long wall, opencast,
  retreat, room and
  pillar, strip

N
natural gas 27
Nigeria 20
nuclear power 6, 34

O
oil 6, 10, 23, 24, 26, 29, 34,
  37
outcrops 10, 18
overburden 18, 19
oxygen 8, 9, 14, 26

P
"pack" 13
peat 8, 9
petroleum 7, 26, 27, 28, 29,
  35, 37
pipelines 23, 33
pithead 15, 36
Poland 6, 20
pollution 30, 35, 36
problems 30-1
pulverized fuel ash (PFA) 29

R
retreat mining 20
Rivesville 34
roadways 12, 13, 20
Roberts Bank Superport 7
roof supports 12, 16, 20
room and pillar mining 20,
  21, 30

S
Sasol Corporation 26, 27
seams 9, 10, 11, 12, 13, 18,
  20
  exposed 10
  inclined 32
Sears Roebuck tower 7
seismic method 10, 11
shafts 12-3, 14, 15, 17
  downcast 12
  upcast 12
  ventilation 12
shearer loader 12, 16
skips 17
slurry 23, 32, 33
South Africa 26, 27
Soviet Union 6, 20, 22, 33
steel 7, 26, 27
  industry 7, 26, 27
  mills 7
strip mining 18-9, 20,
  21, 30, 31
substitute natural gas (SNG)
  27
subsidence 30
Surface Control room 14, 15

T
tars 7, 28
trains 7, 22
  diesel 13
  electric 13
  see also locomotives
transport 36
  of coal 20, 22-3, 33
  of men 15, 22

U
United States of America 6,
  7, 19, 20, 22, 23, 27

W
West Germany 6, 18, 19, 22,
  32

Acknowledgements
*The publishers wish to
thank the following people
who have helped in the
preparation of this book:*
Black Mesa Pipeline Inc.,
British Gas Corporation,
Central Electricity
Generating Board,
Communications and Public
Affairs Department for the
Navajo Power Project,
Phoenix, Arizona, Dr. John
Sharpe, Electricity Council

(Overseas Division), Mining
Research and Development
Establishment, National
Coal Board (Head Office),
National Coal Board
(Midlands Regional Office),
National Coal Association
(U.S.A.), Owen-Luder
Partnership, SASOL ONE
(PTY) Ltd., Sears Roebuck,
The Institute of Petroleum,
World Mining Centre
(Belgium).

Photographic credits:
Page 7, Canadian High
Commission: page 8, David
Bayliss/Rida Photo Library:
page 9, Finnish Foreign
Trade Association: page 12,
COE Metcalf Shipping Ltd.:
page 14, National Coal
Board: page 15, National
Coal Board: page 17, John
Cornwell: page 19, Zefa,
Amax Coal Company: page
20, Compix: page 22,
Gesamtverband des

Deutschen Steinkohlenbaus:
page 25, Central Electricity
Generating Board: page 26,
Utah International Inc., U.S.
Department of Energy,
Sasol: page 30, Zefa: page
31, Spectrum Colour
Library: page 35, National
Coal Board: Endpapers,
Amax Coal Company